Contents

D1252236

The city in its circular fever
repeats and repeats
City, my city,
scorned stela,
dishonored stone.
[. . .]
Patio, wall, ash tree, well
dissolve into a clarity in the form of a lake
A foliage of transparency
grows on its shore. Fortunate
rhyme of peaks and pyramids,
the landscape unfolds
in the abstract mirror of the architecture.

Octavio Paz, *A Draft of Shadows*

Lab Coat Urbanism
Ken Kaplan

Probably the most politically dangerous area of investigation in architecture is imagining new cities. That is why so few architects tender propositions in this area. It is like walking into a chemistry lab with blindfolds on and beginning to pour. Steven Holl has been splashing around in this lab for years, with many corroded lab coats to his credit. In fact, where others, in their so-called theoretical research, reach for distilled water and color dyes, Holl unlatches the lead canisters of the volatile radioactive elements of the periodic chart.

This accounts for the heat and glow of his latest proposal: *Edge of a City*. Optimistic and energy-rich, these projects plant architecture back into the central core of new city visions. While these works easily avoid the familiar trap of conical towers and aspirin-shaped trucks rushing toward fusion-powered sunsets, they also happily evade the currently more common academic papers that define cities as xero-graphic body parts, unclaimed down at the local city morgue. In truth, Holl goes right to the heart of the matter; cities are perceptual acts, precranial laser beams that cut right through the layers of ideological haze. Stitch Plan, Parallax Skyscrapers, and Void Space/ Hinged Space are new cities not because they invent some new park pattern or offer duty-free shops on Main Street, but because they fundamentally attack the way we look out the windows at both the park and Main Street.

Cities are dangerous, but more so are the inventions about them. They cause journalists to sweat. They push window-cleaners into early retirement. Politicians extend their lunch hours to escape seeing them on their desks, or, even worse, outside their office window. Out in their reception area, a grumbling, blackened lab coat urbanist thumbs through moth-eaten back issues of *Pamphlet Architecture*, wipes his nose, and waits.

EDGE OF A CITY

STEVEN HOLL

Princeton Architectural Press, New York
Pamphlet Architecture 13, New York

Edge of a City is part of the exhibition series, "Architecture Tomorrow," curated by Mildred Friedman.
April 21–June 23, 1991: Walker Art Center, Minneapolis
August 22–October 13, 1991: Henry Art Gallery, Seattle

Princeton Architectural Press
37 East 7th Street
New York, New York 10003
212.995.9620

Printed in China
05 04 03 02   6 5 4 3
Publisher: Kevin C. Lippert
Editor: Janet Cross
Assistant Editor: Sarah Dunn
Production: Clare Jacobson
Copy editor: Ann Urban

CIP data available from the publisher
ISBN 1-878271-56-3

Editor's Note

Architecture and city planning today expose only a fraction of the infinite permutations possible in built form. The *Edge of a City* projects just scratch the surface of this potential as imaginary urban schemes designed to respond to extreme changes in recent culture. Though idealistic, they are not "utopian" or without site, as each proposal presents a very different possibility for each specific site.

Inventions rather than solutions, they struggle to defy the prevailing homogeneity of cities, especially at the periphery where sprawling development has an eerie sameness. They aspire to uncover new ways to make cities more habitable, perhaps more beautiful, and to excite change, however indirect.

Throughout these projects, the horizon is a recurring theme. Like tomorrow, it is a paradox, a philosophical construct of eternal anticipation. Yet the notion of a tomorrow is the essence of visionary architecture and planning. Though futuristic schemes are easily stigmatized for their impracticality, even absurdity, change effected by humans must involve contemplation about the future—that which lies beyond the horizon at the edge of a city.

Foreword

The extended twilight of northern cities like Seattle offers a caesura, a silent uncertain suspension for reflective, melancholic thoughts.

Our exploration in this exhibit attempts a celebration of the landscape of natural occurrences, mystery, and transcendent meanings. The phenomenon of place is an objective that can be given new dimensions in the form and material of architecture. Exceptional characteristics of each city have provoked our general experiments in new urban quarters toward the atypical.

I believe that architects ought to undertake research and projects on the scale of the city. The built results of compromised bureaucratic planning processes have presented us with a lack of responsibility in form and quality of life. If speculators and planning agencies are not providing visions, they ought to be challenged. Our architecture and our city plans ought to be cognizant of historical qualities and failures, yet, shouldn't their essence be as different as that of the century before us? With new programs, new challenges, and a fragile landscape to cultivate and preserve, our architecture should, in the words of that great American regionalist, William Faulkner, "Create out of the materials of the human spirit, something which did not exist before."

I would especially like to thank Mildred Friedman, who curated this experiment and allowed us the free opportunity to make a work that asks questions instead of giving answers. Listed in closing are the many people from our office-atelier who worked on this, but, especially, I thank Janet Olmsted Cross for her criticism and untiring help.

Steven Holl, New York, July 1991

Below
Population distribution in
America
One dot represents 1000 people
Facing page
Dallas, Texas

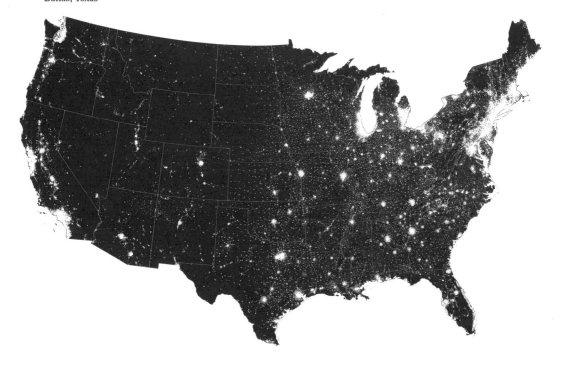

Edge of a City
Steven Holl

The health of the eye seems to demand a horizon.
We are never tired so long as we can see far enough.
Ralph Waldo Emerson

THE EXPLORATION of strategies to counter sprawl at the periphery of cities—the formation of spaces rather than the formation of objects—are primary aims of the *Edge of a City* projects. The expanded boundary of the contemporary city calls for the synthesis of new spatial compositions. An intensified urban realm could be a coherent mediator between the extremes of the metropolis and the agrarian plain.

In each proposal, living, working, recreational, and cultural facilities are juxtaposed in new pedestrian sectors that might act as social condensers for new communities. From "spatial retaining bars" that protect the desert at the edge of Phoenix, Arizona, to void courts that internalize the landscape in Fukuoka, Japan, the six plans entwine with existing circumstances. Though they differ in form, these proposals share a "pre-theoretical ground" of psychological space, program, movement, light quality, and tactility.

ON THE FRINGE of the modern city, displaced fragments sprout without intrinsic relationships to existing organization, other than that of the camber and loops of the curvilinear freeway. Here the "thrown away" spreads itself outward like the nodal lines of a stone tossed into a pond. The edge of a city is a philosophical region, where city and natural landscape

landscape overlap, existing without choice or
expectation.

    This zone calls for visions and projections
to delineate the boundary between the urban
and the rural. Visions of a city's future can be
plotted on this partially spoiled land, liberating
the remaining natural landscape, protecting the
habitat of hundreds of species of animals and
plants that are threatened with extinction.
What remains of the wilderness can be pre-
served; defoliated territory can be restored. In
the middle zone between landscape and city,
there is hope for a new synthesis of urban life
and urban form. Traditional planning methods
are no longer adequate. Looking back at the
city from the point of view of the landscape,
these projects consider untested programs and
new kinds of urban spaces.

    The exponential changes brought about by
air travel over this century exemplify how ex-
periences of space and time change from city to
city. Within hours we are transported from one
climate and time zone to another. Formerly, enter-
ing a city occurred along the earth via a bridge or
a portal. Today we circle over, then jet down to
an airstrip on a city's periphery. Consequently, in
making plans and projections for new city edges,
it is necessary to discard old methods and working habits and begin with basic research.
PSYCHOLOGICAL SPACE is at the core of spatial experience. It is intertwined with the subjective
impression of actual spatial geometry and born
in the imagination. The absolute side of ration-

al planning is in a contrapuntal relationship
with the pathological nature of the human soul.
It is in this mix, at its architectonic conception,
that the spatial spirit of a work of architecture
is determined.

    Sitting in a fishing boat, drifting a few
miles away from the ocean shore, one is surrounded by horizon. Reflections of clouds in
the water double the space of the sky; the
ocean provokes a silent, inward-focusing
mood, psychological as well as spatial. Similar-
ly, the experience of flight, with its views of
space between cloud formations, has a vastness

of dimension that invigorates and excites the imagination. Towers of white clouds bunch independently like cotton skyscrapers. Looking down, the desert floor below seems to be a base for these strange forms. Then suddenly, jet wings cut the towers in half, and the mobile architecture of the clouds is sliced by immense aluminum knives. The spatial exhilaration of air travel has transformed humanity, and the vaporous architecture of clouds has become a phenomenal spatial experience.

The psychic core of a room is like a reverie. The room, an individual's place of periodic repose, either inspires or inhibits creative thought. Insight, fantasies, and imagination are fueled by the psychological space of the private interior.

If we consider the interior as the harbor of the soul, then light, colors, textures, and spatial relationships take on an absolute and urgent importance. The interior, a "psychic vessel of containment," can possess both the clarity and the vagueness required for reflection, fantasy, and passion. The architecture of the interior can alter our experience of time of day or season; it can alter our perception of colors, affecting mood and body temperature. At the direct encounter with interior space, architecture changes the way we live.

Just as the dimension of the soul is depth, not breadth, so the dimensions of an interior may well exist below or above the physical limits of its geometry. Spatial extensions beyond a room's interior—those in a room flanking an open court, for example—may engage and extend the spirit of that interior. Thus spatial projection can be a way of invigorating minimal spaces in housing or in places of confinement such as hospital rooms. IN THE YET-TO-BE-BUILT CITY, notions of passage must be addressed. Consider the city as it might appear in a series of cinematic images: zoom shots in front of a person walking, tracking shots along the side, the view changing as the head turns. At the same time, the city is a place to be felt. Notions of space, shifting ground plane, plan, section, and expansion are bound up in passage through the city. Consider movement through the city framed by vertical buildings. Each change of position reframes a new spatial field. This parallax of overlapping fields changes with the angles of the sun and the glow of the sky. Premonitions of unknown means of communication and passage suggest a variety of new urban spaces.

In the modern city the voids between buildings, not the buildings themselves, hold spatial inspiration. Urban space is formed by vertical groupings, terrestrial shifts, elongated slots of light, bridges, and vertical penetrations of a fixed horizontal. Urban space has a vertical Z dimension equal to, or more important than, the horizontal X–Y plane. This perpendicular spatial order is amplified by a range of viewpoints from various levels. From a roof terrace, a subway platform, the upper floors of a tower, or an underpass, vertical urban perspective is experienced on a shifting ground plane.

The experience of parallax, the change in the arrangement of surfaces defining space due to the changing position of the viewer, is transformed into oblique planes of movement. Spatial definition is ordered by angles of perception. THE INCREDIBLE ENERGY in such cities as New York, Milan, and Paris is related to programmatic diversity and juxtaposition. Modern metropolitan life is characterized by fluctuating activities, turbulent shifts in demographics, and changing desires of restless populations.

We do not call for a new disordered architecture to match the disorder of culture; such duplication simply affirms the chaotic, and achieves no other dimension. Rather, we propose experiments in search of new orders, the projection of new relationships. This is not meant to

Top to bottom
Oil exploration—after the
detonation of a seismic charge
Clothes line
Neutrino reaction

transpose our study into a system or method, and yet the energy inherent in the development of new relationships presents us with a continuity of ordering that inspires reflection.

Consider the experience of reading a comprehensive morning newspaper, an ordering of life in society. The following untenable juxtapositions might be paralleled in urban terms: an article describing a billion-ton floating island of ice that is drifting around the North Pole is next to an article about the construction of a twenty-four-foot-diameter water tunnel and a piece on the austerity program of a religious cult. Alongside a column on insomnia and the sleep movement of plants is a huge diagram of the "Pacific Rim" trade network. An article on Japanese factories in Mexico is adjacent to a photograph of a hole in the ozone layer over the South Pole.

To precisely translate thoughts and feelings sparked by incredulous relationships is as problematic as translating an English word into all of the world's 2,796 languages. Precision of the rational gives way to intuition; subjective dimensions establish physical dimensions.

A spatial arrangement, an aroma, a musical phrase may be imagined simultaneously. Depending on the awareness and imagination of the perceiver, an initial visual field can provoke subject matter and imply programs. We can speak of the sounds implied by an array of brittle linear forms, or by the way a view smells. An individual's cultural associations,

Top to bottom
Transferred across fields
Program = natural phenomena +
evidence of causes + suspension
Rightful autonomy

recognition of materials and imagination of
their properties, and the physiological effects
of space and enclosure all present individual
limitations. The perceiver's angle of vision and
preconception are potentially open to the ad-
hesion of unforeseen associations. Rather than
allowing prejudice to be a primary subjective
determinant, one can induce associations by increasing the possible number of programs to oc-
cupy an urban setting.

Isolated buildings of a single function, the
suburban norm, typical at the modern city's
periphery, give way in these projects to hybrid
buildings with diverse programs. An effort
toward programmatic richness—an open association of spaces to program suggestions (action
images)—is fertilized by gathering and juxtapos-
ing a variety of activities.

The *Edge of a City* projects probe phenomenological dimensions in the formation of new
urban spaces, in order to transform the tangled
waste at the fringes of our modern cities and
build new urban sectors with programmatic
spatial and architectural richness. Beyond this
horizon we are seeking a moving territory between the extremes of idea and physical experience. In the same way that the French
philosopher Maurice Merleau-Ponty suggested
that the "absolute separation of meaning from
factual existence in every region of experience
is in fact impossible," any constructed space
can be defined by its first inhabitant—a psychological space, whether of angst or joy.

Below
All the canals of Milan—past and present
Facing page, top to bottom
Site: Porta Vittoria
Section through Botanical Garden
Subway Station

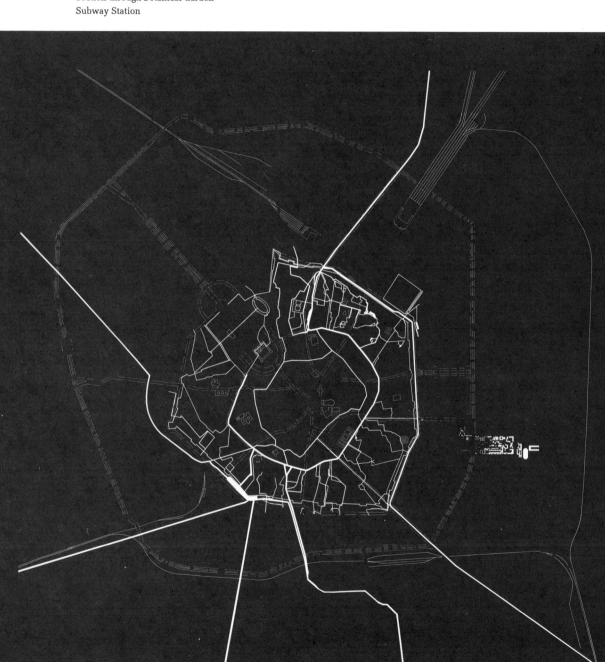

Milan, Italy
Porta Vittoria

In this project for the reuse of the Porta Vittoria rail yard in Milan, commissioned by the XVII Triennale of Milan, free association—"semi-automatic"—programming is a strategy for increasing diversity and juxtaposition.

From a dense center, Milan unfolds in circles ringed by a patchwork grid that finally sprawls raggedly into the landscape. Against this centrifugal urban sprawl (from dense core to light periphery), a reversal is proposed: light and fine-grained toward the center, heavy and volumetric toward the periphery. This proposal projects a ring of density and intensity, adjoining the rolling green of a reconstituted landscape.

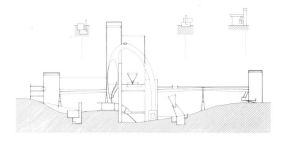

The site for this project is a freight rail yard, now in disuse (part of the old railroad belt around Milan), bordered by blocks of various kinds of housing. It fronts onto Largo Marinai d'Italia, a ragged park on land reclaimed from a poultry and vegetable market.

A new strategy for urban morphology is explored; instead of an *a priori* plan projected later into perspectives, perspective views of overlapping imagined urban spaces are drawn and projected backward into plan fragments. With the help of a sectional "correlation chart" these space fragments are adjusted to form a whole city sector where interdependent characteristics of programs and building sections are intensified. Diverse building sections and program relations form a prepositional chart suggesting the intrinsic intersection of programs as a bonding, fastening, or disjunctive force.

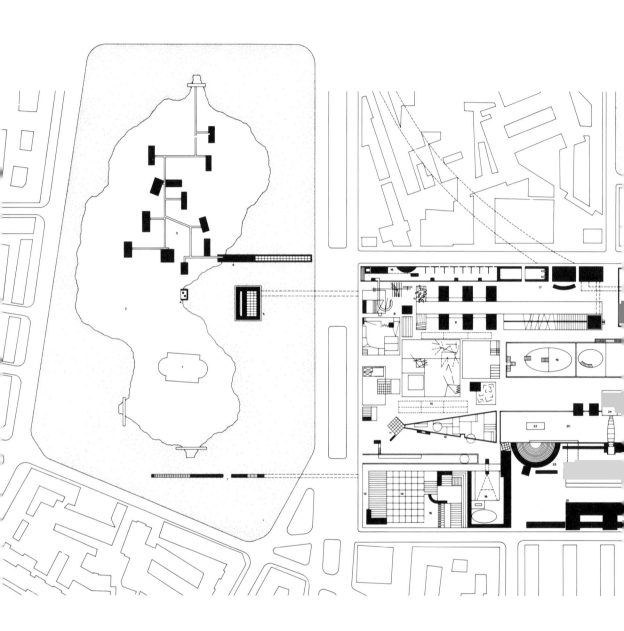

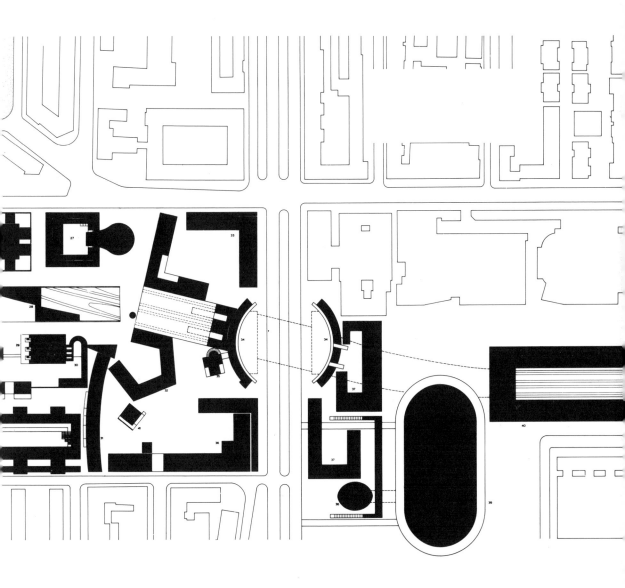

22. Jack-Up Rig/Stage
23. Amphitheater
24. Lovers' Hotel/Psychological Bridge
25. Correlating Facility
26. School of Humanities
27. Museum with Cinematic Insertions
28. Shear Workshops

29. Delegate Interview Switchback
30. Three-Lobbied Neck/Archival Library
31. Bureaucratic Double-Flux Slab
32. Four-Sided Pentagon
33. Interlocking Office/Housing
34. Passante Train Station/Shops
35. Control Tower/Administration

36. Corner Hotel/Offices
37. Office Block
38. Air Terminal/Ticketing
39. Bus Garage/Velodrome
40. Parking Garage/Switching Booth
41. House of Appeals and Petitions

Left
Passage below Water Basin
Right
New Subway Station opening
onto Elongated Gap

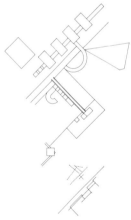
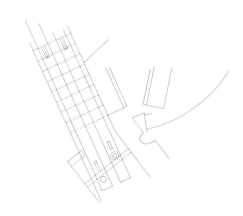

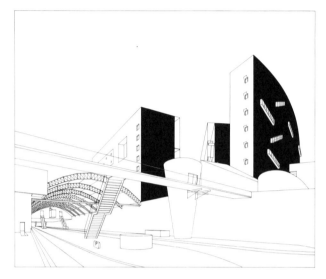

Left
Garden of Sounds
Right
View at Elliptical Passage

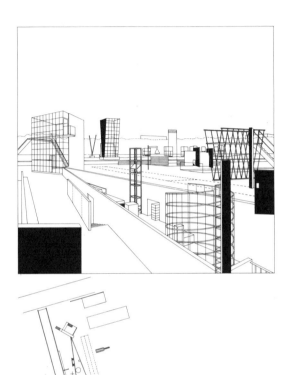

Left
Diagonal view across Residential Court
Right
View from court of Four-Sided Pentagon

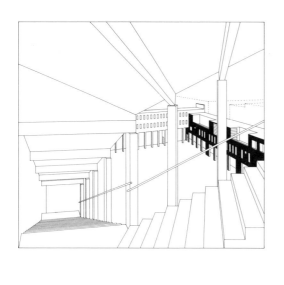

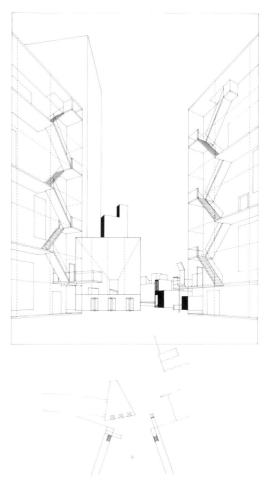

Left
Three-Lobbied Neck/Archival Library
Right
Water Basin, Amphitheater, and
Jack-Up Rig

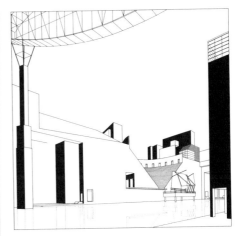

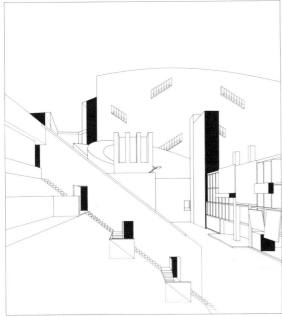

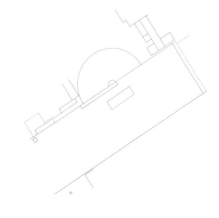

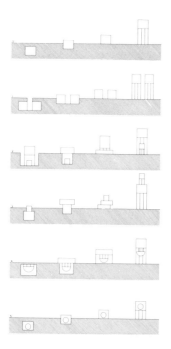

0	Primary relations
1	Near
2	Over
3	Atop
4	Under
5	Within

6	Against
7	Between
8	Through
9	Across
10	Beside
11	From

1	Under within a within (below)
2	Over within a within (below)
3	Atop an under (below)
4	Atop a from (below)
5	Over a through (in)
6	Against an under (in)
7	Under a between (in)
8	Across (on) over a through (under)
9	Atop a vertical through (in)
10	Through a beside (in)
11	Across an atop beside (on)
12	Atop an across (in)
13	Within a through (on)
14	Through a from (on)
15	Through atop (on)
16	Within atop (on)
17	From a within through (on)
18	Atop a between (on)
19	Above near from a within (on)
20	Within a from beside (above)
21	Over an against (on)
22	Against an over (above)
23	Across against a from (above)
24	Under an across (above)

Six partial models in alignment
over site plan

Below
Cleveland site map with "stitches"
Facing page, left
Chessman Dam, Colorado
Facing page, right
Model of hybrid dam

Cleveland
Stitch Plan

Five *X*s spaced along the inland edge of Cleveland (the northern edge is formed by Lake Erie) define precise crossover points from new urban areas to a clarified rural region. These newly created urban spaces are girded by mixed-use buildings.

At one *X* the crossover is developed into a dam with hybrid functions. The urban section contains a number of buildings including a hotel, a cinema, and a gymnasium. The rural section contains public programs related to nature, including a fish hatchery, an aquarium, and botanical gardens.

The artificial lake formed by the dam provides a large recreational area and extends the crossover point into a boundary line. Taken together, the *X*s imply an urban edge.

Axonometric of hybrid dam,
site plan, and building section

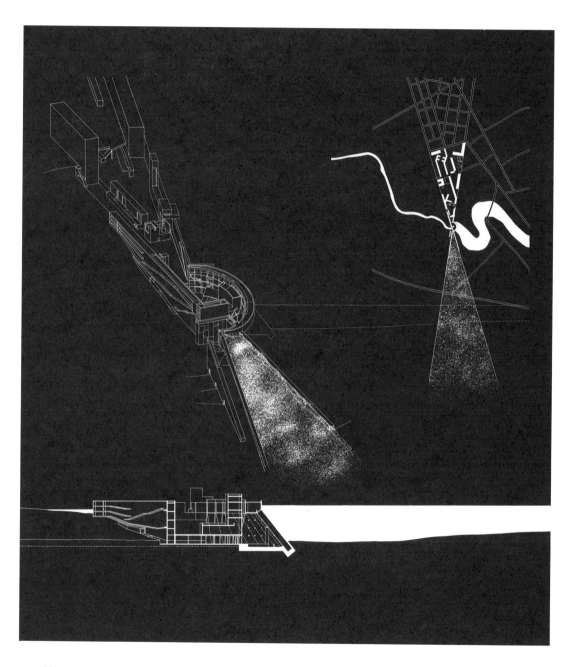

Cleveland horizon with *X*

Phoenix
Spatial Retaining Bars

The most prominent aspect of the history of Phoenix is the mysterious disappearance of the Hohokum Indian civilization after their cultivation of the valley with 250 miles of thirty-foot canals for 1000 years.

Sited on the periphery of Phoenix, a series of spatial retaining bars infers an edge to the city, a beginning to the desert. Each structure inscribes a 180-foot-square space while it rises to frame views of the distant mountains and desert.

Loftlike living areas hang in silent isolation, forming a new horizon with views of the desert sunrise and sunset. Communal life is encouraged by entrance and exit through public squares at grade. Work is conducted electronically from loft spaces adjoining dwellings. Cultural facilities are suspended in open-frame structures.

The thirty-foot-square building sections act as hollow, reinforced concrete beams. Exteriors are made of pigmented concrete with the undersides of the arms polished to a high gloss. In the morning and evening these undersides are illuminated by the red desert sun—a hanging apparition of light once reflected by the water of the Hohokum canals.

Top
Worm's-eye view
Bottom left
Interior axonometrics
Bottom right
Site plan

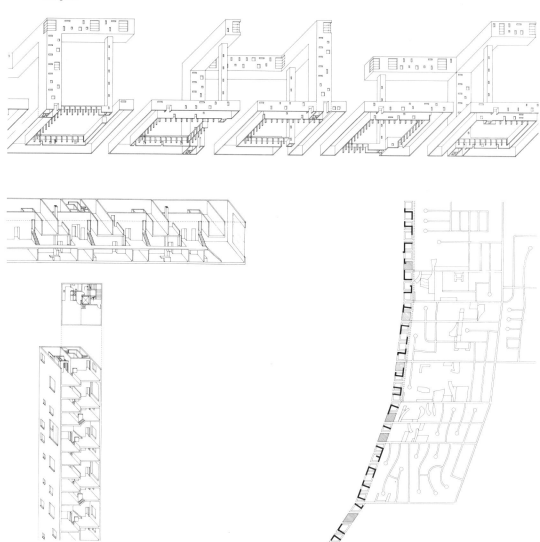

Section model of courtyard building

Manhattan, Penn Yard
Parallax Skyscrapers

In this proposal, the existing 72nd Street train yards would be transformed into a new city-edge park in the spirit of Frederick Law Olmsted. The existing dense development to the east looks out over this new open park, which extends to the Hudson River's edge.

On the river, ultrathin skyscrapers bracket the view and create a new kind of framed urban space over water. Hybrid buildings with diverse functions, the towers are linked by horizontal underwater transit systems that connect underwater parkside lobbies to high-speed elevators serving upper transfer lobbies. Occupants are within walking distance of the 72nd Street subway entrance or express ferries to the Jacob K. Javits Convention Center, Wall Street, and La Guardia Airport.

In counterbalance to the ultrathin towers, an ultrathick floating public space is used as a concert stadium, large-screen movie theater complex, or grand festival hall.

Below
Dallas–Fort Worth
Spiroid sectors with protected prairie
Map of Texas
Facing page, top
Freeway loop; edge of Dallas

Dallas-Fort Worth
Spiroid Sectors

Protected Texas prairie is framed by new sectors that condense living, working, and recreational activities. Future residents are transported to new town sectors by a high-speed MAGLEV transit from the Dallas–Fort Worth Airport.

A new hierarchy of public spaces is surrounded by armatures knotted in a continuous space-forming morphology. Various public passages along the roof afford a shifting ground plane, invigorating the interconnected experience of the sector's spaces.

The coiling armatures contain a hybrid of macroprograms: public transit stations, health clubs, cinemas, and galleries, with horizontal and vertical interconnected transit. Micro-programs of domestic activities are in smaller adjacent structures. The smallest spiroids form low-cost courtyard housing in experimental thin/thick wall construction.

Spiroid sector site diagram

___ Dallas Fort Worth freeway system
▨ Protected Prairie
🞙 Spiroid Sector
····· MAGLEV transit: 200 mph

Seven stations:
1. Black Snake
2. Anima Mundi
3. Breakwater
4. Sanctuary
5. Campus
6. Hangdog
7. Instantaneity

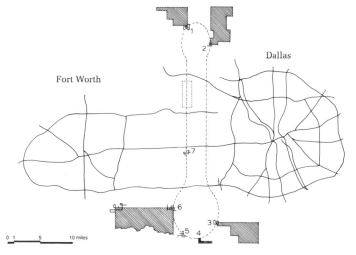

Large spiroid model with beam
of pure planar construction

Pure planar construction,
exploded axonometric

Top
Provisional housing model within
large spiroid construction
Bottom
Provisional housing plan

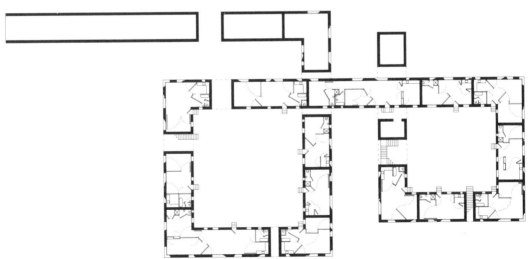

Institute of Science
Plate tectonics and tornado machine
Spiroid sector, building type "A"

MAGLEV station, public spaces, and cinema
Spiroid sector, building type "A"

Facing page, top
Site plan: a new quarter of the city was built in eleven months by six architects working separately on a diagrammatic plan drawn by Arata Isozaki.

Architects
(counter-clockwise from left):
Steven Holl, Rem Koolhaas, Mark Mack, Osama Ishiyama, Christian de Portzamparc, and Oscar Tusquets.

Facing page, bottom
Light passing through void spaces
Below
Bay of Fukuoka, Japan, with site plan insert

玄海灘

博多港

福岡湾

福岡市

Fukuoka, Japan
Void Space/Hinged Space Housing

Four active north-facing voids interlock with
four quiet south-facing voids to bring a sense of
the sacred into direct contact with everyday
domestic life. To ensure emptiness, the south
voids are flooded with water; the sun makes
flickering reflections across the ceilings of the
north courts and apartment interiors.

The flooded voids are in fact still ponds,
which are a phenomenal lens, capturing the
light of the sky and the changes in brightness
over the day. Looking down into the ponds,
one can see clouds or occasional aircraft passing overhead. The bottom of the ponds have
the same smooth black rocks as those used in
the game of "GO." A measure of weather, the
ponds ripple in the wind and fill with circles of
raindrop patterns. The dry voids on the north
interlock in section to allow the passage of the
sun and views through the building section.
The body of the building, being more than fifty
percent void, focuses its intention not on the
concrete, but on nothingness.

Interiors of the twenty-eight apartments
revolve around "hinged space," a development
of the multiuse concepts of traditional *fusuma*
taken into an entirely modern dimension. One
type of hinging—diurnal—allows an expansion
of the living area during the day, to be reclaimed for bedrooms at night. Another type—
episodic—reflects the changes in a family over
time: rooms can be added or subtracted to ac-
commodate grown-up children leaving the
family, or elderly parents moving in. A third

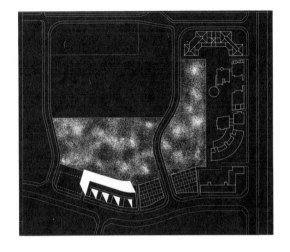

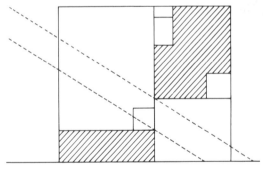

Top
Passage along water court
Bottom
Apartments above water court

type of hinged space—seasonal—allows walls to be adjusted to react to the path of sunlight and to the path of wind through the apartment.

The hinged space engages each inhabitant in manipulating and changing the nature of interior views and space. The individual positioning of the "participating walls" causes rooms to appear or disappear.

One of the most important aims of housing in the wake of the failures of modern-movement housing projects is to introduce the humanizing dimension of individual differences. Here, each of the twenty-eight apartments is unique. Individuality is inwardly, rather than outwardly, expressed. The complex interlocking in section allows each apartment many exposures looking north, south, east, and west. Morning, afternoon, and evening light can be fully felt.

An experiential sense of passage through space is heightened in the three types of access that allow apartments to have exterior front doors. On the lower passage, views across the water court and through the north voids activate the walk spatially from side to side. A sense of suspension with the park in the distance occurs along the north passage. The top passage has a sky view under direct sunlight.

The change in movement and perspective is increased by the curve of the building plan. A series of walkways suspended on thin steel rods connects the three passages vertically across the north face. This heightens the spatial

Top
Units interlock in plan and
section, interconnecting the
different court spaces

exhilaration of movement, acting like steps
along the face of a stone cliff.

At each end is a lobby: on the east is the
everyday lobby with postboxes and a colored
plaster wall/floor mural depicting "hinged
space." Partially rotating glass planes and
hinged-glass light fixtures further activate this
lobby. On the west is a special terminal lobby, a
place for reflecting on the end of the everyday.
It has white plaster walls and ceilings and a
pure white marble floor. A "catafalque" bal-
cony has "piping" of a single black steel line.

The structure is exposed bearing-wall concrete with eight concrete columns—one for
each void space. While walking along the street
from west to east, one sees the structural bear-
ing wall with a few small, sliced windows.
While walking from east to west, an entirely different series of side facades shows a sectional
cut through the building with lightweight
aluminum infill panels. A blue-green stain on
the facade expresses the planar nature of the
structure and the street edge alignment.

The building, with its street-aligned shops
and simple facades, is seen as part of a city in its
effort to form space rather than become an architectural object. Space is its medium, from urban
space to paired voids to interior hinged space.

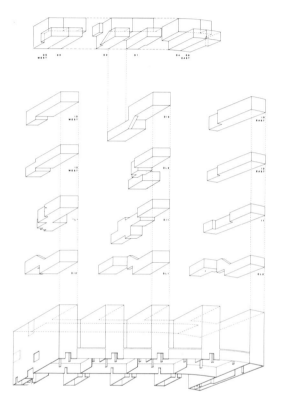

Street facade

Model view of rear facade:
a study of the passage of light
through the void spaces

America: Realism and Utopia
Stan Allen

*Those who maintain that New York is ugly are
simply the victims of an illusion of the senses.
Not having yet learnt to move into a different
register, they persist in judging New York as a
town, and criticize the avenues, parks and mon-
uments . . . The beauty of New York has to do
not with its being a town, but with the fact, obvious once we abandon our preconceptions, that
it transposes the town to the level of an
artificial landscape in which the principles of
urbanism cease to operate, the only significant
values being the rich velvety quality of light,
the sharpness of distant outlines, the awe-
inspiring precipices between the skyscrapers
and the somber valleys, dotted with multi-col-
ored cars looking like flowers.*

Claude Lévi-Strauss, *Tristes Tropiques* (1955)

*Everybody has their own America and they
have pieces of a fantasy America that they
think is out there but they can't see.*

Andy Warhol, *America* (1985)

IN STEVEN HOLL'S *EDGE OF A CITY* exhibition, despite the presence of projects for Japan and
Italy, and without endorsing superficial region-
alisms, it seems important to underline the
"Americaness" of the works presented. In each
of the projects, perhaps most evidently in
Holl's *Spiroid Sectors* (1991) proposed for
Dallas–Fort Worth, the constructed presence at
the edge of the city is reinterpreted as "artificial landscape," where the "principles of

urbanism cease to operate" precisely because
they have become obsolete.

Reflecting on the condition that has in-
creasingly dominated the exurban territory of
American metropolitan regions, Holl offers cri-
tiques and corrections. Not without nostalgia
for a dense, coherent urbanism, he paradoxi-
cally finds an unprecedented freedom of opera-
tion from the lack of available formal models.
In the Dallas–Fort Worth project, he has proposed a vast new quarter in spiral form, in-
tended both to mark the limit of the city and to
fold the landscape into these urban quarters.
Lévi-Strauss's intuition—that in America the
conventional distinction between town and
landscape no longer pertains—inspires a new
hybrid, neither of the city nor of the landscape,
but drawing positive characteristics from each.

With the project for Dallas–Fort Worth,
Holl realizes his ambition to create "spaces
rather than objects." The *Spiroid Sectors*, con-
necting the city centers and the airport, produce a density of services within a spatial con-
figuration, which could only exist in this
undefined territory at the edge of the city. The
spiral form, fundamentally open and unfinished, complements the horizontality of the
landscape and provides unexpected moments
of spatial intimacy and programmatic intensity.
Critical of the separation of functions enforced
by modern zoning, Holl imagines a mixed-use
quarter incorporating housing, transport termi-
nals, research institutions, and public spaces.

Top
Robert Smithson, *Spiral Jetty*
(1970)
Bottom
Robert Smithson, *Amarillo
Ramp* (1973)

The project explicitly addresses issues of transportation, from air travel to new forms of mass transit, adding credibility to the scheme. The viewer—or inhabitant—of *Spiroid Sectors*, like that of its most obvious precursor, Robert Smithson's *Spiral Jetty* (1970), needs to move into a new perceptual register to comprehend its spatial form.

Holl's research here parallels Rem Koolhaas's recent investigations. Koolhaas has also looked at the periphery of the American city (Atlanta, in his case) as a source of new urbanistic strategies. He takes note of the economic and social realities that have created these new spaces, which are neither properly urban nor really natural. He sees new opportunities here: "It is clear that Atlanta itself is not producing great architecture, but it is impossible to go there without being excited by the potential of how impressive this architecture could be if some developments were interpreted with more virtuosity." The changes that have accompanied these new developments may not be explicable in terms of currently available formal models; he describes a "city without the classical symptoms of an urban situation, without any density . . . a city in the sense of its facilities." In the tradition of Frank Lloyd Wright's dream city of infinite horizontal extension, another form of city has emerged, but now based on new economic and social realities such as working mothers and the electronic cottage industry.

In *Edge of a City*, Steven Holl has taken the exhibition format as an opportunity to comment critically upon these and other existing urban realities. The exhibition has a didactic and propositional tone. His critique takes the form of concrete alternative proposals, suggesting that architecture still has something to contribute to the shape of the city. Thus the Manhattan *Parallax Towers* (1990), an unsolicited, alternative proposal to the massive overdevelopment of the West Side rail yards, investigates the space-defining conditions in the city and produces an unexpectedly suggestive urban complex.

It is worth noting that this preoccupation with the form of the American city is not something new for Holl. In research previously published in the *Pamphlet Architecture* series, i.e., *Alphabetical City* (1980), he attempted to transcribe European research of typology and urban form into a specifically American context. The *Gymnasium Bridge* (1977), which won Holl early recognition, was a fundamentally urban invention, an unexpected insertion into the structure of the city. Therefore, it is not surprising that he has revived and extended this research in the present exhibition, notwithstanding the reputation he has gained in the meantime as a careful and modest constructor.

It is not for me to ponder what is happening to the "shape of a city," even of the true city distracted and abstracted from the one I live in by force of an element which is to my mind what air is supposed to be to life. Without regret, at this moment I see it change and even disappear.
Andre Bréton, *Nadja* (1928)

THROUGHOUT THE PROJECTS exhibited here, Holl works to extend the phenomenological ground that has been the basis of much of his earlier, small-scale work to large-scale urban form. This is a difficult task inasmuch as the delicate phenomenological layering, the "psychological space" (movement, light quality, and tactility) proposed as a "pre-theoretical ground," does not easily translate to the incisive, propositional quality of the best of the work here. In an effort to bridge these scales, Holl proposes a phenomenology of the limit: "This zone calls for visions and projections to delineate the boundary between urban and rural." These projects set out to mark, contain, or announce this boundary. But the privileged ground of individual perception, the interior as a "psychic vessel of containment," a liminal zone of barely registered perceptual shifts, cannot be so directly translated to the socially produced and politically mediated limits in the space of the city. Too much of the vitality and complexity of the city must be bracketed out in order to achieve this moment of private insight.

Thus in some of the earlier projects presented here, this attempt to extend the phenomenology of the limit to the urban realm leads to a certain rigidity. For example, the Cleveland *Stitch Plan* (1989) proposes literal and metaphoric figures of containment: a dam and the separation of functions by the imposition of a new geometry in order to produce a "new urban area" and a "clarified rural area" (a place that may have already disappeared).

In the Phoenix *Spatial Retaining Bars* (1989), the theme of restraint becomes even more explicit. In the Western landscape, the twin figures of horizontal extensivity—the road and the desert—have created an unmapable, unmeasurable space. This is a characteristically American landscape, which cannot be contained within familiar forms of urban space. The space of the desert is described by Jean Beaudrillard as an embodiment of America's mythic view of itself: "Here your eye can no longer properly settle on things, and all human or natural constructions that intercept your gaze seem irksome obstacles which merely corrupt the perfect reach of your vision." The perfect architecture of the desert would be an invisible architecture, a stealth architecture, an architecture on the verge of disappearance. Here is perhaps the thread that links Lissitsky's *Cloud-Prop* (1926) to the lost canal system of the Hohokum Indians, who inhabited Phoenix before the white settlers. The never-realized avant-garde dream appears as a geometric mirage from which to view the shimmering reflection of a long-vanished culture.

Yet to concentrate solely on the literal sense or even the psychological content of any document to the sore neglect of the enveloping facts themselves circumstantiating it is just as harmful; etc.
James Joyce, *Work in Progress* (1928)

EXHIBITIONS HAVE BECOME a major aspect of the public and professional discourse on architecture today. In part, this is the result of renewed attention directed to architecture and design under the extended gaze of a commodity-based culture. In addition, the exhibition has become attractive as a surrogate to building, given the actual shortage of building opportunities. Architecture is thereby displaced into the realm of the culture industry, with all its limitations and built-in affiliations.

This exhibition sets distinct terms for its reading. It revives an instrumentalist paradigm of exhibition, taking over its didactic and informative qualities, but reprogramming its assumed objectivity. These projects are not to be read as literal (and fully developed) proposals but as propositional sallies into the urban realm. The diagrammatic quality that they exhibit is consistent with this intention. Quite deliberately, the ideas are unfinished; the

Top
Superstudio, *Continuous City*,
(1972)
Bottom
Raymond Hood, *Residential
Bridges* (1929)

viewer is induced to read into the projects and fill in the empty slots. They belong to a tradition of utopian realism like that of Superstudio and Yona Friedman in the sixties and the Japanese Metabolists in the fifties; they recall Raymond Hood's *Residential Bridges* and Le Corbusier's urban proposals of the twenties and thirties. As with other architects working in this tradition, there is something seemingly arrogant in Holl's assuming the power to remake the image of the city. Yet this is the territory in which these projects operate most effectively: not as concrete proposals, but as infiltrations of the collective imagination, producing an idea of what the city could be. And it is here that their effect may actually be felt—not in the realization of one or two interventions, but in the incremental and cumulative changes in the horizon of possibilities in the contemporary city. Working in a territory from which architects have, in general, withdrawn themselves, Holl presents these projects primarily as images—broad outlines of an idea whose details will be fleshed out through complex but disparate means. We have to take it on confidence that, if developed, these projects might acquire the density of the Fukuoka Housing project, the one built project illustrated here.

Holl's use of large-scale photomontages as the preferred presentation medium is the best evidence of this "utopian realism." Despite the delicate, framed watercolors scattered throughout the exhibition, there is a consistently

grainy black-and-white tone to this exhibition. Unique to the photomontage is its capacity to conjoin the most radical degree of abstraction with the most extreme degree of realism. This contrast of extremes is deployed with clear strategic intent. A cadence of pristine volumes organized by an inviolate geometry, for example, is threaded through the stubby trees and grimy highways of Cleveland's industrial periphery. This coupling of the highly abstract and the evidently realistic underlines both Holl's exhibition strategy and his propositional stance. In scale the montages are roughly the size of a person. The viewer apprehends them with the body; there is something cinematic about their space. Moreover, mounted on canvas and hung loosely from the wall, they become objects in themselves, not simply representations. Yet, unlike the watercolors, they are not unique handmade objects, but the serial products of mechanical reproduction.

Nor is the redefinition of exhibition strategies limited to graphic means. The Dallas–Fort Worth model/object dominates the exhibition space as construction. It works both as installation, modifying the spatial experience of the gallery, and as didactic device, an explication of the proposal. The installation operates in several scales simultaneously: a model for the organization of the territory, a walk-through exhibit of an individual sector, a sectional detail at the intermediate scale, and a full-scale demonstration of the proposed method of construction.

Without limiting himself to a single paradigm of exhibition, Holl has freely deployed available strategies to reinforce his intention. Thought at the level of the city overrides any other exhibition concept. The idea of the exhibition is therefore bigger than the exhibition itself. As a result, the form of the whole is sometimes difficult. In his best moments, Holl turns over and reprograms the current social and formal reality of the city's periphery, allowing us to see the landscape of the American city in a new way and offering a powerful critique of present patterns of the occupation of this still undefined zone. Accepting the potential for failure, he has made an entry into this difficult territory. And if the discipline of architecture is not to become even more marginalized than it is at present, it must rise to the challenge of this space "at the edge."

—review of *Edge of a City* exhibition, May 1991
revised for publication

Installation view of *Edge of a City*
Walker Art Center, Minneapolis, 1991

Credits

Project team for *Edge of a City*:
Hideaki Ariizumi
Laura Briggs
Steven Cassell
Sarah Dunn
Scott Enge
Tod Fouser
Hal Goldstein
Thomas Jenkinson
Peter Lynch
Jennifer Murray
Chris Otterbein
Adam Yarinsky
Christopher Cosma, cast glass
David Dick, installation construction
Janet Cross, exhibition coordinator
Special thanks to Larry Rouch
and Lebbeus Woods

Major funding for *Architecture Tomorrow* has come from the Jay Chiat Foundation, The Graham Foundation for Advanced Studies in the Fine Arts, and Helen and Kim Whitney. Additional support for the Fukuoka portion of the exhibition was provided by Ken-ichi Toh of the Fukuoka-Jisho Corporation.

Cover image, Elliot Erwitt (Magnum), from Jean Beaudriuard, *America* (London: Verso, 1988).
Inside cover, Aerial Photomaps, Dallas, 1989.
p. 5, Photo/Chronicles, Ltd., New York, 1987.
p. 9, Doug Tomlinson, *Dallas Architecture, 1936–1986* (Austin: Texas Monthly Press, 1985), p. 127.
p. 13, Andreas Feininger, *The Face of New York: The City as It Was and as It Is* (New York: Crown Publishers, 1954), p. 43.
p. 14m, The Albertype Co., Brooklyn.
p. 14b, Tony Hey and Patrick Walters, *The Quantum Universe* (Cambridge: Cambridge University Press, 1987), p. 147.
p. 15t, Courtesy Morgan & Morgan Inc.; from *Encyclopedia of Source Illustrations*, 1972.
p. 15b, André Kertész, 1927.
p. 17t, Milan Trienalle, 1987.
p. 17b, Susan Wides.
p. 27l, *Landmarks in Civil Engineering* (Cambridge: MIT Press, 1987), p. 253. Reprinted with permission of American Society of Civil Engineers.
p. 57t, Nancy Holt, *The Writings of Robert Smithson* (New York: New York University Press, 1979), p. 109.
p. 57b, ibid, p. 204.
p. 58b, ibid, p. 88.
p. 60t, Superstudio, *Arthropods* (New York: Praeger, 1972), p. 97.
p. 60b, Giorgio Ciucci, Francesco D'Alco, and Mario Manieri-Elia, *The American City* (Cambridge: MIT Press, 1979), p. 460.

Pamphlet Architecture was initiated in 1977 as an independent vehicle to criticize, question, and exchange views. Each issue is assembled by an individual author/ architect. For information, pamphlet proposals, or contributions please write to Pamphlet Architecture Ltd., 37 East 7th Street, New York, New York 10003.

Pamphlet Architecture is distributed exclusively by Princeton Architectural Press, 37 East 7th Street, New York, New York 10003. Telephone: 212-995-9620

Pamphlets published:

1. Bridges	S. Holl	1978*
2. 10 California Houses	M. Mack	1978*
3. Villa Prima Facie	L. Lerup	1979*
4. Stairwells	L. Dimitriu	1979*
5. The Alphabetical City	S. Holl	1980
6. Einstein Tomb	L. Woods	1980*
7. Bridge of Houses	S. Holl	1981*
8. Planetary Architecture	Z. Hadid	1981*
9. Urban and Rural House Types	S. Holl	1983
10. Metafisica Della Architettura	A. Sartoris	1984*
11. Hybrid Buildings	J. Fenton	1985
12. Building; Machines	R. McCarter	1987
13. Edge of a City	S. Holl	1991
14. Mosquitoes	K. Kaplan/T. Krueger	1993
15. War and Architecture	L. Woods	1993
16. Architecture as a Translation of Music	E. Martin	1994
17. Small Buildings	M. Cadwell	1996
19. Reading Drawing Building	M. Silver	1996
20. Seven Partly Underground Rooms	M. Ray	1997
21. Situation Normal	Lewis. Tsurumaki. Lewis	1998
22. Other Plans	Michael Sorkin Studio	2002

*Out of print, available only in the collection *Pamphlet Architecture 1–10*